matsu·kaze

poems

karen mireau

Azalea Art Press
Southern Pines . North Carolina

ISBN: 978-1-943471-04-1

Cover and Interior Art
by Carol Van Zandt

for
all the lost children

Other Titles by Karen Mireau

The Conscientious Visitor
with Marla Lay

Marienau: A Daughter's Reflections
with Dr. Annemarie Roeper

Sweet Land of Liberty: 50 Years Later
with John A. Wedda

Contents

Introduction

The poetic work contained in this volume is so fresh and astonishing that it defies easy categorization. More like a symphony with twenty-two movements than a collection of separate poems, **matsu•kaze** is a work that impacts us on many levels, especially when read in its entirety, and Carol Van Zandt's original sumi ink brush paintings amplify the emotional power of the poetry. Through the spontaneity and subtle interplay of light and dark in each painting, we sense the movement of emotion and nature even before we experience the poems themselves.

In **matsu•kaze**, Karen Mireau has created a masterful poem cycle held together by lyrical language, themes of suffering and redemption, vivid imagery of very specific birds and trees and landscapes, and deep insights into the links between the human spirit and the natural world. As one poem states, "it is the nature of children and poetry to shift our attention to that not easily seen." This collection opens our vision to let in more of everything that whispers in the forest of our souls as we are guided to make sense of our own woundedness. It's as if nature is both witness and healer along this path, with the internal and external worlds merging and separating in a dance where we are continually becoming lost and found.

Beauty, birdsong, the steadiness of trees, and open-heartedness in the face of loss are the compass points that help Karen Mireau navigate through these poems, and deep wisdom and compassion are the rewards of the heroine's journey she so generously shares with us. She has clearly "learned the language of feather, forest, cloud / the exalted arias of sky and bird," and we are all the richer for hearing it spoken here.

I am profoundly grateful that Karen Mireau has allowed these poems to flow through her and into us, her fortunate readers. Because the poem cycle elevates my perspective and expands my humanity, as only the most inspired art can do, I will carry **matsu•kaze** in a sacred corner of my heart as I move through life. I invite you to experience the realm of **matsu•kaze** for yourself. Prepare to be moved and changed.

– Cynthia Leslie-Bole, M.A.
Founder, Hummingwords Writing and Coaching

matsu · kaze

wind in the pines

shirataki : a thousand rainsticks
the percussion
of a waterfall, far off

> *some hear it as a roaring*
> *an amplified hush*

a river of whispers
spreading through the forest
quieting the birdsong

> *woodpecker, wren*
> *siskin, jay, thrasher, all fall silent*

as if they, too, are awed
by the musicality of pine tassle
turning in the wind

> *a symphony of crushed ice*
> *a sea of shattered chimes*

the longleafs, towering above
a chorus of ancient lullabyes
sweeping the Sandhills sky

> *oh how bittersweet it all is*
> *to recall our innocence*

the child in us naturally tuned
to the spirit voice in the trees
so clear, so very clear

> *we must stop, look up*
> *in perpetual wonder*

hekishoku : green darkness
the sound of invisible fire
coursing in the canopy

    what awakens
    what calls our soul-self forth

wetted wind
lifting from the glassine surface
of Powell Pond

    the mysterious path
    once lost, now found again

longleaf pine canopy
swaying in contrapuntal circles
a carousel of leafy hands

    knowing, not knowing
    the dance continues

crows, a murder of them, arrive
syncopated, singular
then, silent

    equilibrium
    disequilibrium

first light
the color of buttermilk
clouds in absentia

    a chevron of charred wings
    crossing the now almost-apricot sky

seika : sacred melody
the fox-colored wood thrasher
is said to sing three thousand songs

>   *imagine*
>   *the unimaginable*

that a bird
could have a repertoire
that vast

>   *breath taking*
>   *breathmaking*

how does it learn all this
in such a short life?
a decade, at best

>   *spent on the edge*
>   *of the striated understory*

elusive troubadour
calling out its doubled phrases
from a high branch

>   *"plant a seed"*
>   *"plant a seed" s/he begins*

some deeper mystery
repeated in its serious stance
the teardrops on its striped belly

>   *an unaccountable, inhuman strength*
>   *radiating from its brilliant yellow eye*

shousui : greyness, grief
a slow rain falls, a shroud
over longleaf pine boughs

> *we have all felt so much pain*
> *so much sorrow*

the pines are witness
sifting the skyfall with equal measure
softening the earth below with ochre shadow

> *everything comes*
> *everything goes*

when my father died
I made a pilgrimage to my favorite pine
and buried his name there

> *green and purple leaf mold*
> *enveloping the last of him*

that tree, a sturdy guardian
for four centuries or more
and patient witness

> *to the black, untended scars*
> *the thick bark that covers shame*

it had seen enough of us
to know that we have
our own tap roots

> *in need of angry tears*
> *to grow deeper, more real*

komorebi : sunlight
filtering like butterflies
through pine needles

if drops of rain are tears
then sun shadows are warm kisses

some early mornings
they occur together —
lovely, temporal paintings

pure imprints of light
impossible to recall completely

the mind tries
and tries again
to hold onto that most sacred

to rewrite the past
recast the future

even as a child I knew
art was necessity
it was everything, salvation

an imperfect dance between sun, shadow
love, anger, and sometimes, forgiveness

perhaps this is what we all do
within the memoir of damage
to find a place of surety

to keep that worth keeping
redefine truth, what is truly true

kagetsu : bright moon
the whole air thick with ghosts and angels
the water music of early April

dreamy, sensory centrifuge
for the sleep-starved brain

trees swaying and circling
cascading this way, that
sometimes in tandem, often not

on such a night
what enters our dreams, unannounced?

an invisible bird
singing the same note
unceasingly in the dark

trees mired in green moonlight
a battered calliope of leaves

to which we all are drawn
willingly, achingly
desiring the delirium

spinning round and around
up and down, to that old music

the mothers who never came for us
the fathers who made us take a name
never really ours

we children, wide-eyed, waiting impatiently
to ride far beyond it, tickets in hand

shoshun : early spring
everything unhinged
dogwood buds break open

first green spears
stab the bright morning

unfold into starry cups
blood-tipped sepals and orbs
thrust into glistening lemony stamens

they know
they, too, know despair

at seeing such beauty
kaleidoscoping again and again
over a single tree, an entire terrain

there comes a time
when we can barely stand it

the air all flowers
inescapable, this perfume of life
contrapuntal to darkness, death

the entire universe
dancing, a choir of dogwood

round and round
always it comes to this
ecstatic, suicidal moment

and then, the comforting embrace
of those irrepressible optimists, the azaleas

matsukafun : pine pollen
the warmth of April wind
releasing the clustered catkins

curtains of pale gold dust
drifting over the pond

blanketing rooftops, roads
kissing the fields
with ochre powder

painting everything
with a sexual glow

we're all drunk on pollen grains
love-sick, veering into spring
on a heady dose of fertilization

monoecious, each tree
both male and female

pollen a love food
an aphrodisiac
in Native American lore

the red conelets open, receive
are impregnated then fade to yellowish-green

two years later the seeds mature
then, abra-ca-dabra
the cones reopen, release

the next generation
adrift on the wind, seeking a new home

mikkoku : betrayal
the last I heard, he was dying
but that may have been a lie, too

> *sociopaths are like that*
> *saving the most hideous torture, just for you*

I'll admit that I loved him
and yes, I knew why
but that never stopped me

> *just as it doesn't stop the abuser*
> *or the vulnerable from being abused*

we're encouraged from birth
to crave that familiar echo
the doppleganger of our youth

> *yet it takes just one enlightened witness*
> *only one — to realize this is true*

there were others I loved with my whole heart:
the poet who died of cancer when I was sixteen
the rock singer who drank himself into oblivion

> *and my dear red-headed friend, Burdock*
> *who hung himself from a crossbeam*

oh, those unspeakable abandonments
I still grieve —
for having left me alone on this old earth

> *then ripe, once again*
> *for the picking*

seishi : history
is kind if you know how to tell it
purely, without all the bullshit

> *to bypass what you've been told*
> *go straight to what is true*

this, then, is my story
I was born a slender stem
but later I grew bark

> *I needed protection then, though I've grown*
> *stronger and much more kind to myself*

I've seen enough destruction
of the spirit
to last a lifetime, yet also

> *magic, wonder, mystery*
> *the glimmer of a white violet in the woods*

and more than my fair share
of children and their laughter
what could be better, richer than that?

> *those things, these things*
> *become everything*

when you are starting from scratch
praying to the trees for just another day
in which to live your life

> *without the unspeakable thought*
> *of having to start all over again*

11

shinzui : essence
what will we really have learned
at the end of things

> *what will we care about*
> *who will love us*

tend to our failed bodies
our ruined faces
our imperfect memories

> *what will remain of meaning*
> *of our life story, then?*

it would seem
there are two kinds of people
at every phase of life

> *those who seek happiness, and those*
> *who know it only exists in the moment*

I have friends over ninety
who tell me how hard it is
to depend solely on others

> *and others who thrive*
> *on the attention they've always craved*

our beloved trees bear witness to this
our longing and striving
our giving and taking, loving and doubting

> *the unending human refrain — can you hear it?*
> *a spell-bound calling, the wind in the pines*

matsukasa : the cone
wrapped tight and smooth
as a riverstone

> *a whorl*
> *a helical world unbounded*

viewed from the top
a mandala
exactly balanced on its axis

> *where the wooden scales*
> *are sprung – a fibonacci spiral*

bracts opening, closing
seed scales emerging at pollination
protecting the two-year old embryos

> *each bract a sharp prickle*
> *a hook to hug the forest floor*

purplish males
the smaller pollen bearers
only females capable of birthing

> *but first must come fire*
> *to clear the mineral ground*

a screen of smoke
a spin of the dial, a tumble
through the crapshoot of space and time

> *to a place where life, enlightenment*
> *may or may not take root*

koboku : old tree
I put my palm to your auburn bark
ragged, ravaged by many fires

> *sentinel to five hundred years*
> *of North Carolina life*

your own tap root
as deep as ten meters or more
wide as your three-foot trunk

> *all from one small miracle*
> *one seed, determined to flourish*

the older we are, the more difficult it gets
time escaping almost unnoticed
a wing slipping through the pine boughs

> *and there you are*
> *the years flown*

longleaf incantations
whisper in the pines
like the Santa Anas back west

> *and I make a childish wish*
> *while the doves banter and coo*

that like them
I may find a place I could know
and truly be known

> *a place, just one place*
> *to call my very own*

marasame : autumn rain
a sprinkling of ash
a showering of smoke and flame

the longleaf
forged by fire from the beginning

the burning of understory
over thousands of years
a ritual secret of its survival

allowing seeds to release
the forest to flourish

also blazing a trail
for the turpentiners
who invaded the heart of this country

scarring the trees
with "cats faces" for miles and miles

deep V's cut to drain the gum
for naval stores, sold cheap
to fuel the British Navy

trees pillaged, then logged
until almost all were gone

this history sustained the people
bound and blinded them
to the souls of the trees

the longleaf will never be the same
this blackened rain, we pray, will never return

setunai : pining, longing
as a small child
there were trees most dear to me

maple, oak, elm, hickory
each one a living reverie

a druid baby, hours upon hours
I hid in their branches
dreaming that I could fly

the leaves, the green wind
my cloak of invisibility

there I learned the language
of feather, forest, cloud
the exalted arias of sky and bird

each note, each phrase
a new wing

taking me far, far away
where no one could wrest from me
the solace of imagination

the birds —
they knew what awaited me below

but never spoke of it
saying only
'stay,' 'stay,' 'do stay'

until only thirst, my new kitten's cry
might finally coax me down

kitsutsuki : woodpecker
silence broken by sudden cartoonish laughter
a sweep of endangered wings

>   *'a knock at the door by the knock-knock bird'*
>   *my three-year-old granddaughter observes*

and there, high up in the longleaf
a rarity –
the Red-Cockaded Woodpecker

>   *it is the nature of children and poetry*
>   *to shift our attention to that not easily seen*

in the old days it was said
a squirrel could leap from branch to branch
for mile upon mile and never touch ground

>   *of ninety-two million acres*
>   *only three million now remain*

the insistent thrumming, once so familiar
now corralled
to these diminished patches of piney woods

>   *in these times*
>   *this is one of the things we must grieve*

our human greed, our failure
to see the world with the eyes of a child
each bird a miracle

>   *may we all live to see something better*
>   *come of it*

meiro : labyrinth
I walk for hours
and cannot find my way

> *I've left a trail of crumbs*
> *but the crows have eaten them all*

crumbs were all I had
for so long
and now they, too, are gone

> *there is only the outline of the trees*
> *the murmuring of black water nearby*

frogs that burble and bleat
like strange sheep in the night
some amphibious, hallucinogenic flock

> *this goes on and on*
> *then suddenly, stops*

now I am really lost
awake or asleep
no bearings any longer

> *this is what comes*
> *of having no map*

of starting down the trail
into the interior, the thick of it
with only dead stars to guide you

> *when the sun, that hidden door, swings opens*
> *nothing is as it once was*

matsubayashi : pine forest
the sound of softened footfall
muffled pinestraw beneath your boot

    each time you step into a pine grove
    these things are present

undocumented memory —
the embrace of a lover who died long ago
the face of a child you will never know

    what is and what might have been
    are initials carved in the same tree

can you remember, old poet
what it was like to whirl
about together in the newly-fallen snow

    making angels, stealing kisses
    under the frozen pine boughs

or riding the old carousel
in the fog of our first, and last, autumn
before your death?

    residing deep in the heart
    these things can never be erased

the pine stands symbol
a cross, a bridge to the bridled past
that can never be shaken from me

    no matter where I go
    no matter which way I turn

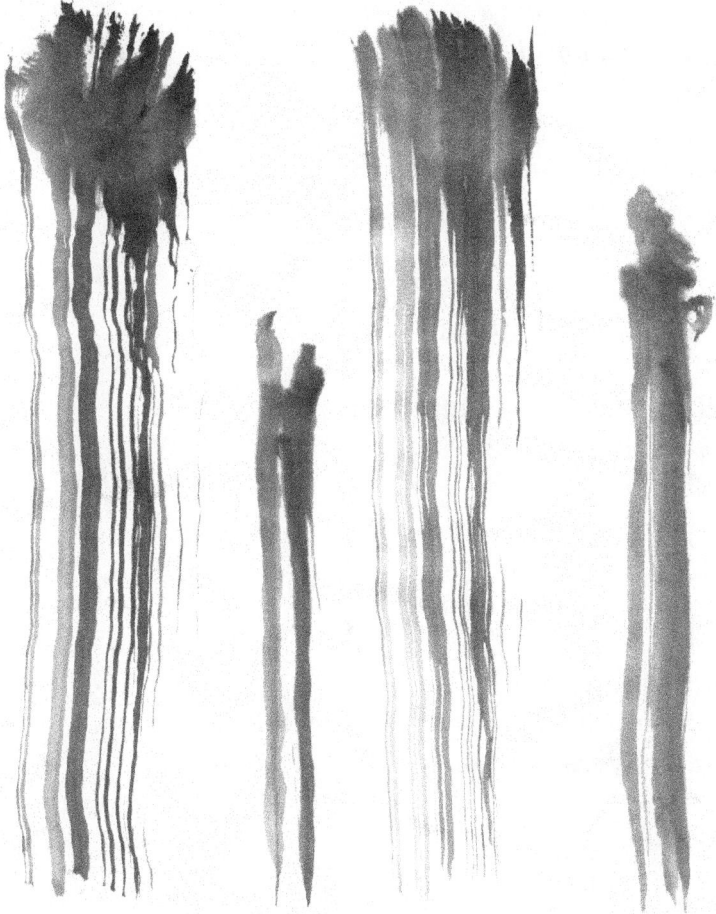

utaguri : uncertainty
we are all plagued by anguish
from time to time

> *lost in the forest*
> *of our own choosing*

there comes a moment
when the life we sought to live
seems illusory at best

> *how we got from there to here*
> *an atlas of emptiness*

a delicate ambrosia of *if's*
that even if left unspoken
is undeniable to ourselves

> *the bend in the river*
> *the fork in the road*

that questioning is never far
from the dreams we might have followed
when we were young

> *and so it goes*
> *and so it goes*

our regrets forge our future
what is left behind
allows us to transform

> *each day the trees stand by*
> *patiently forcing our eyes toward heaven*

hangetsu : half moon
a white bowl filled with the song
of nightbirds

> *a circle made of dreams*
> *undreamt, about to find voice*

in the calliope of pines
the mouths of the mockingbirds
that are poised to speak

> *heralding both beauty and terror*
> *on the edge of morning*

a lullaby of memory and loss
soft as the interior
of a moonflower

> *receptacle of white light*
> *a cup full of stars*

a nursery rhyme
repeated over and over
to the daughters we longed to know

> *their faces a litany*
> *of the ones that never came to be*

and so, we make an offering
to the moon goddess
to the mystery, to the futility

> *of our own flawed life*
> *of our failure to love our fragile self*

21

inabikari : flash of lightning
night sky obscured by red clouds
thunder drawing near

> *soundless cannon fire*
> *pummeling the far horizon*

loneliness, she said
is when our radiance
finds no purpose

> *this is your task —*
> *to discover why you are here*

each teacher arrives
each lesson given until it is learned
for some of us it just takes longer

> *oh, so often I did not see it*
> *in my case, almost sixty years*

there is no longer shame in that
no longer any fear
of what may come

> *I now see who I am*
> *who I was and who I might be*

my heart in gratitude
filled with praise
for the gifts I've been given

> *illumination rains down*
> *fast and sweet as silvered pine blood*

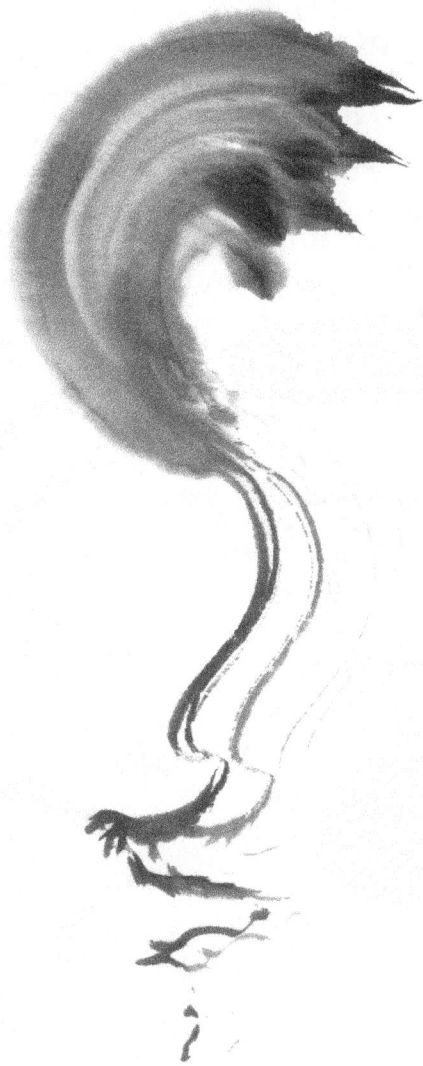

keika : firefly light
the space between two pines
an entry to a new world

this is where I live now
between this, between that

each day begun in gratitude
each day ending in sheer wonder
at my survival

it's not as strange as it seems
to be a dreamer, many are

there is an advantage
to seeing things from the other side
or, more often, inside out

it goes without saying
you know your place

to give, to be kind
to know deeply
to touch and be touched

all these gifts are given
who is to tell you otherwise?

it will be the same
no matter where you are
or who you might be among

the path is simple and absolutely clear
love, dream — dream, love

Author's Note

matsu•kaze was composed—or more accurately, channeled—over a one-month period that coincided with the anniversary of the death of my father. Each morning, a poem emerged in its entirety, and it was as if I was being handed a small, luminous gift to assist me in the final phase of my grieving.

Just as miraculous to me was the offer by Carol Van Zandt to illustrate the poems. Carol's experience in Asian brush painting and calligraphy made her a perfect match for the sensibility of **matsu•kaze**. That creative interplay became central to the development of the book you now hold in your hands. She is truly my partner in the birthing of **matsu•kaze** and my gratitude to her is boundless.

Upon the excellent advice of my editor, Cynthia Leslie-Bole, the sequence of the poems was altered slightly to clarify the flow of the poem cycle; otherwise the text is basically as it was set down. We resisted the

impulse to over-edit the poems, with the intention of preserving the rawness of the emotion and inspiration.

For several years I had been living in "the piney woods" in the midst of one of the last remaining tracts of ancient longleaf pine forests, in the Sandhills region of North Carolina. My life at that time was pared down to a zen-like simplicity. The Japanese words in **matsu•kaze** flowed from that mindset, as well as from the very soulful, nurturing trees that surrounded me.

My letting go of "things" during this period was followed by what I can only describe as a decluttering of my mental landscape. I spent my time primarily in the *pinus palustris* woods, listening to the birds and closely observing the plants and animals in this very special eco-system. Slowly, I began to reimagine the trajectory of my life in a very different way.

This was further catalyzed by twenty-four months of intensive trauma therapy. I was very fortunate to find a highly gifted therapist in Jennie Rose, who gently and methodically "re-parented" me and brought me to a place of personal healing. It was probably the most difficult and humbling two years of my life, but shortly after, when the poems in **matsu•kaze** began to surface, I knew that I had arrived at a very different place, and my profound sense of renewal was magnified by being among the longleafs.

The spiritual nature of these trees is never more evident than when the wind is coursing through the forest canopy. From far off, I could hear the sound of dreams being born and feel my soul being swept clean by a music that could only be conjured by "the wind in the pines." The next phase of my journey had truly begun.

– Karen Mireau

Karen Mireau is a Literary Midwife and founder of Azalea Art Press who has helped authors manifest their literary vision for over thirty years. Karen began her life as a full-time poet. She went on to create animated children's television, raise a family of enormously artistic children, and to become a committed "agricultural anarchist" on her organic farm, where she cultivated over three-hundred varieties of heirloom fruits, flowers and medicinal herbs. She has now has returned to her first love—poetry. **matsu•kaze** is her first full-length collection of poems.

Artist's Note

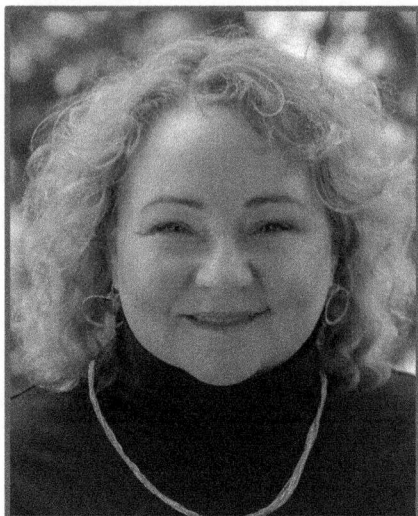

When I read **matsu•kaze** and considered creating images to go with Karen Mireau's poems, I was transfixed. I wanted to capture the feeling the poems evoke and have them dance on the page in conversation with the words.

The journey portrayed in **matsu•kaze** is ethereal and transformative, with the forest a place of revelation and healing, letting go, and emerging. These are some of the things I wanted to express. I didn't want to confine readers to a certain conclusion by suggesting literal visualizations, but rather use gestural images — many of them one-stroke paintings — to provoke and allow them to experience the poems in a more open-ended way.

I used traditional *sumi* sticks, Japanese brushes and handmade Japanese paper. As I rubbed the *sumi* stick against the inkstone to create the ink, I would read the poems and then meditate. When the ink was ready, I then

would be ready as well to paint from a place of not thinking. It has been a wonderful process, and I am so grateful and honored to have collaborated with Karen Mireau on this project.

– Carol Van Zandt

Carol Van Zandt holds a BA in Studio Art from Boston College and studied at Massachusetts College of Art, Rhode Island School of Design, and The Institute for Textile Print Design in California. Carol spent ten years studying calligraphy and sumi painting. Her eastern art influences were further developed during her seven-year residencies in Tokyo and Taipei. An exhibiting artist for many years, her paintings are in private collections in over fifteen countries in Europe, Asia and America.

Acknowledgments

**Honor must be given
to all of the muses and midwives
who assisted in the birthing of this book.**

My creative partners:

Cynthia Leslie-Bole
My beloved sister-friend and creative collaborator —
for these things and for your unerring editorial eye,
I owe you my literary soul. Your generosity,
your indefatigable spirit and ever-present faith
and encouragement to me have been gifts
that defy any earthly definition.

Carol Van Zandt
As my childhood friend, there is always our shared
history to be grateful for — but I am equally appreciative
of this merging of our creative paths in our later lives.
The power of your art in this book is beyond anything
I could possibly have imagined and I thank you with all
my heart for making **matsu • kaze** a beautiful reality.

My literary and artistic rock:

Patti Edmon
Each day, I meditate with overflowing gratitude
for the beauty and depth of our friendship — one that has
witnessed and shared almost a half-century of life
challenges. This book contains the essence of our twin
desire to be free of the past and to continue to
express ourselves fully as vibrant, creative women.

My grandmothers:

Jeanne C. Fletcher
(1910 - 1988)
My paternal Grandmother gently cultivated
my knowledge and respect for dimensions other than
this one. Her ability to see beyond the veil of illusion
taught me much about the potential of poetry
to awaken and change our view of the universe.

Kathryn Mignon Garlock
(1905 - 1990)
Always a source of feminine power and inspiration to me,
my maternal grandmother's love of art, music and the
natural world forged my own awareness of how to
deeply listen and to attend to the stories in the trees.

My mother and soul-mothers:

Alma Hurley Johnson
(1919 - 2004)
There are times when you know without question
that you have met an Angel. Alma was truly one
here on this Earth. Her love and care for all beings
will always be deeply impactful and inspiring to me.

Cynthia Garlock Kozlowski
My mother has always been a source of creative counsel
and artistic support. She has been a powerful example
of how to weave art into everyday life with integrity.

Dr. Annemarie Roeper
(1918 - 2012)
Annemarie profoundly influenced my growth as an
individual and as an artist. The memory of her strong,
loving and innovative spirit is always present
in my heart. She will always be my soul-mother.

My spiritual guides:

Dr. Gabriele Jones
Dr. Jones' support has been critical to my healing journey. Her steady patience and skills in EMDR and Neuro-Optimal feedback have been key factors in opening the doors to deeper insight.

Marylinn Kelly
As a true sage and visionary, my dear friend Marylinn has been instrumental in guiding me through over forty years of creative and personal ups and downs. I am continually in awe of her ability to see, to define and to artfully express the truth in so many media.

Marla Lay
Marla's irrepressible spirit and boundless compassion have been a constant source of illumination to me. Her nurturance of others while facing her own daunting personal challenges is a beautiful example of how love and faith can transcend all.

Jennie Rose
I will forever be grateful to Jennie Rose. Her expertise as a life and trauma therapist helped me navigate through what seemed like an impenetrable emotional forest. Her loving guidance along the sometimes rocky path to wholeness was the major catalyst for this book.

Marina Mendez Williams
From the time she was conceived, my daughter has been my greatest inspiration. Brave, wise, and infinitely creative, she has taught me many life lessons. I am forever grateful for her honesty and her ability to embrace life so fully and so deeply.

My creative sisters:

Ann Bowe
Ann has been a dear friend and literary supporter
for over a decade, as well as my partner
in appreciating the birds of the woodlands,
especially the magical, mystical woodpecker.

Darlene Dunham
Dar's friendship and generosity of spirit
have been a constant source of literary and moral
support. My thanks to her for being there for me.

Susen Hickman
As a first reader of the manuscript, Susen's
insights as a sister poet were invaluable to me.
My deep gratitude to her for responding in such
a positive, encouraging and enlightened way.

Miyuki Irie
Miyuki's contribution to this book has been essential.
Without her knowledge, I would not have had the
confidence to weave the Japanese terms that were so
specific and necessary to the poems into the text.

Lisa Mitchell
Lisa's love and respect for all the beings that inhabit
this planet are evidence of her earth-mother-spirit.
As she travels the globe carrying her message of peace,
friendship and understanding, she encourages
all of us to do the same in our own work.

Mary Tuchscherer
Mary's enthusiasm gave me the added confidence
to bring this book to fruition. Thank you, Mary, for your
sweet sensitivity and for the magnificent work you do
as the founder of VoiceFlame to bring
the gift of writing to the women of Malawi.

My father and soul-grandfathers:

George H. Johnson
(1916 - 2012)
George's kindness and care for all the children—
including myself and my daughter during a time
when we very much needed his guidance—made him
a most admired and beloved part of our life.

Richard W. Kozlowski
(1931 - 2013)
When we began working together on my father's
biography, I soon realized how little I really knew of him.
He died before were were able to complete his story—
and my grieving for him and all we had lost
was the genesis of the poems in **matsu • kaze**.

John A. Wedda
(1911 - 2014)
Special acknowledgment must be given
my dear friend John Wedda— author, fine artist,
environmental and political activist—whose life has
become my template for living an involved, loving
and purposeful life.

About the Longleaf Pine

Prized for their tall, straight timber and their byproducts of turpentine resin and other naval stores, the longleaf pines (*pinus palustris*) were a valuable commodity for export in early America.

Ninety-two million acres of majestic old-growth forests of longleaf pines once flourished over 150,000 square miles, from southeast Virginia to the Florida peninsula to east Texas, but in the space of 150 years were nearly obliterated to fuel the demands of the British Navy.

The remaining stands of longleaf forest in the Sandhills region of North Carolina are the epicenter of biodiversity in the South, with a long list of plant species and endangered animals and birds, like the Red-Cockaded Woodpecker, found nowhere else on Earth.

Fortunately, the longleaf pines are now being protected and re-propagated by associations such as the Weymouth Woods Sandhills Nature Preserve, the Sandhills Area Land Trust (SALT), the Walthour-Moss Foundation and The Longleaf Alliance. With awareness and a helping hand from us, the magic and beauty of the longleafs will continue to be enjoyed by future generations.

To reach the author, please email her at
Azalea.Art.Press@gmail.com.

For events and commentary, please visit
http://matsukazepoems.blogspot.com.

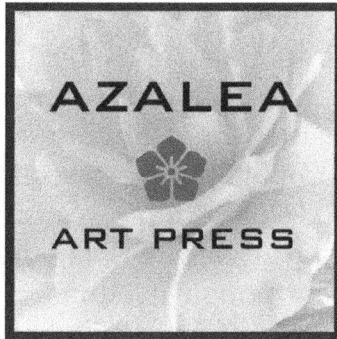

AZALEA

ART PRESS

For more about Azalea Art Press, please visit
http://azaleaartpress.blogspot.com.

To order books, please contact
www.Lulu.com.

www.ingramcontent.com/pod-product-compliance
Lightning Source LLC
Chambersburg PA
CBHW031140270326
41931CB00007B/635